T0209894

From Alpha to Omega

Our God Is an Awesome God!

Jenifer Hosch

WestBow Press books may be ordered through booksellers or by contacting:

WestBow Press
A Division of Thomas Nelson & Zondervan
1663 Liberty Drive
Bloomington, IN 47403
www.westbowpress.com
1 (866) 928-1240

ISBN: 978-1-4908-8154-6 (sc)
ISBN: 978-1-4908-8155-3 (e)

Library of Congress Control Number: 2015908065

Print information available on the last page.

WestBow Press rev. date: 6/8/2015

WESTBOW
PRESS
A DIVISION OF THOMAS NELSON
& ZONDERVAN

Dedication

This ABC book is dedicated to my wonderful family!

**Thanks to my husband, Jon,
my children and their spouses,
and my 12 grandchildren!**

Introduction

Revelation 1:8: "I am the Alpha and the Omega", says the Lord God, "who is, and who was, and who is to come, the Almighty." The first letter in the Greek alphabet is Alpha, and the last letter is Omega. God was telling us that He is the first and last of everything.

I love ABC books! I taught elementary school for 32 years. In that time, I used so many beautifully illustrated ABC books in my classroom. Sometimes, I asked my students to make their own ABC books about the subjects we had studied. They made ABC books about nouns, verbs, geography, history, etc. I found that this was a good way to get them to think about what they had learned. As I read Revelation 1:8, it occurred to me that God is EVERY letter in the alphabet, and I began to think about creating an ABC book about God.

I also love to take photographs when I travel. One day, as I was reading my Bible, I came upon a verse that made me think of a photograph I had taken in Wyoming. I remembered how I felt that day. I was overwhelmed with the beauty of the breathtaking scene I was viewing! I was humbled by the awesomeness of God's creation! I found other photographs of places that had given me that same euphoric feeling!

Romans 1:20: "For since the creation of the world God's invisible qualities- His eternal power and divine nature- have been clearly seen, being understood from what has been made, so that men are without excuse."

I spent the next two years taking photographs of places that clearly displayed God's greatness. I decided to use my photographs to create an ABC book about God and His creation. I know that many of you have taken pictures of places and felt this same awe. I hope you enjoy my personal praise to the Creator, and see "God's eternal power and divine nature" in these pages. I encourage you to create your own ABC book about God.

Psalm 19:1: "The heavens declare the glory of God; the skies proclaim the work of His hands."

*Since I have never traveled into space, I wish to thank NASA for two of the photographs from space in my book.

A a

Our God is
AWESOME!
He is ABLE to
ANSWER our prayers.

Psalm 47:2 "How awesome is
the Lord Most High, the great
king over all the earth!"

2

3

B b

Our God is
BENEVOLENT.
He BLESSES those
who BELIEVE
in Him.

Psalm 112:1 "Praise the Lord. Blessed
is the man who fears the Lord, who
finds delight in His commands."

4

C c

Our God is the
CREATOR who
CARES for us and
COMFORTS us.

Nehemiah 9:6 "You alone are the Lord. You made the heavens, even the highest heavens, and all their starry host, the earth and all that is on it, the seas and all that is in them. You gave life to everything, and the multitudes of heaven worship you."

6

D d

Our God is DIVINE. He DELIVERS us from evil and opens the DOOR to eternity.

Romans 1:20 "For since the creation of the world God's invisible qualities- His eternal power and divine nature- have been clearly seen, being understood from what has been made, so that men are without excuse."

E e

Our God is ETERNAL. His love ENDURES from EVERLASTING to EVERLASTING.

Deuteronomy 33:27a "The eternal God is your refuge, and underneath are the everlasting arms."

Ff

Our God is our
FATHER in Heaven,
our FRIEND who
FORGIVES our sins.

Psalm 86:5 "You are forgiving and good, O
Lord, abounding in love to all who call to you."

G g

Our GOD is GRACIOUS, GENTLE, and GOOD.

Isaiah 30:18 "Yet the Lord longs to be gracious to you; He rises to show you compassion. For the Lord is a God of justice. Blessed are all who wait for Him."

H h

Our God is HOLY.
He is our HELPER
and HEALER.

Psalm 99:5 "Exalt the Lord our God and
worship at His footstool: He is HOLY."

I i

Our God is IMMORTAL. His ways are INDESCRIBABLE and INCOMPARABLE.

1 Timothy 1:17 "Now to the King eternal, immortal, invisible, the only God, be honor and glory for ever and ever. Amen."

J j

Our God is JOY! He is JUST in all His JUDGMENTS.

Psalm 66:1 "Shout with joy to God, all the earth!"

20

Kk

Our God is KING. He is KIND and He KEEPS His promises.

Daniel 4:3 "How great are His signs, how mighty His wonders! His kingdom is an eternal kingdom; His dominion endures from generation to generation."

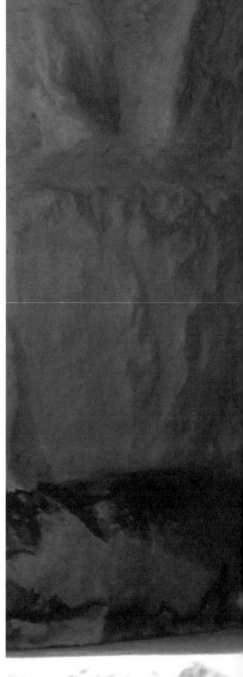

22

L l

Our God is LOVE. He is the LIFEGIVING LIGHT of the world.

John 3:16 "For God so loved the world that He gave His one and only Son."

M m

Our God is MAJESTIC! He is our MERCIFUL MASTER.

Psalm 8:1 "O Lord, our Lord, how majestic is your name in all the earth! You have set your glory above the heavens."

27

N n

Our God is NOBLE.
He sends good NEWS
and NAVIGATES
our way.

Psalm 29:2 "Ascribe to the Lord the
glory due His name; worship the Lord
in the splendor of His holiness."

O o

Our God is
OMNIPOTENT.
He OPENS his
Arms and OFFERS
us His love.

Luke 1:37 "For nothing is
impossible with God."

Pp

Our God is POWERFUL! He is PATIENT and PERFECT in every way.

11 Peter 1:3 "His divine power has given us everything we need for life and godliness through our knowledge of Him who called us by His glory and goodness."

Qq

Our God is
QUOTABLE.
He is with us in
QUIET moments and is
QUICK to comfort us.

Proverbs 30:5 "Every word of God is flawless;
He is a shield to those who take refuge in Him."

Rr

Our God is **RIGHTEOUS**. He is our **ROCK** and our **REFUGE**.

Psalm 119:137 "Righteous are you, O Lord, and your laws are right."

S s

Our God is
SPLENDID. He is
our SHEPHERD
who SAVES us
from our enemies.

Psalm 96:6 "Splendor and majesty
are before Him; strength and
glory are in His sanctuary."

T t

Our God is TRUSTWORTHY. He TENDERLY TEACHES us what is right.

Proverbs 3:5 "Trust in the Lord with all your heart and lean not on your own understanding."

U u

Our God is UNIQUE. He is UNSURPASSED in His UNDERSTANDING.

Isaiah 40:28 "Do you not know? Have you not heard? The Lord is the everlasting God, the Creator of the ends of the earth. He will not grow tired or weary, and His understanding no one can fathom."

43

V *v*

Our God is
VICTORIOUS!
He is *VIRTUOUS*
and *VIGILANT*
in everything.

Psalm 45:4 "In your majesty ride forth victoriously in behalf of truth, humility and righteousness; Let your right hand display awesome deeds."

44

W w

Our God is
WONDERFUL!
He is WISE and
WORTHY of praise.

1 Chronicles 16:9 "Sing to Him, sing praises
to Him; tell of all His wonderful acts."

X x

Our God is
EXHALTED. He is
EXTRAORDINARY
in power and
EXCELLENT
in understanding.

Psalm 108:5 "Be exhalted, O God, above the
heavens, and let your glory be over all the earth."

Yy

Our God is
YAHWEH,
who YEARNS
to be our God and
YIELDS to no one.

1 John 3:1a "How great is the love
the Father has lavished on us, that we
should be called children of God!"

Zz

Our God is the ZENITH of all things, gentle as a ZEPHYR, and ZEALOUS for our good.

11 Samuel 7:22 "How great You are, O Sovereign Lord! There is no one like you, and there is no God but you, as we have heard with our own ears."

53

Our God is an Awesome God! Study Guide

One exciting way to praise God, the Alpha and Omega, is by using the alphabet to plan 26 days of your personal Bible study. Read about these Bible characters, and see how they followed God in their lives, and how God can work in your life!

A- Abraham's prayers were ANSWERED when our AWESOME God was ABLE to give him a son in his old age! (Gen. 12:1-3; 21:1-7)

B- Barnabas, who BELIEVED in Jesus Christ and accompanied Paul on his first missionary journey, was BLESSED even in persecution by our BENEVOLENT God. (Acts 4:36; Acts 13-14)

C- Cornelius, a Gentile, was CARED for by our great CREATOR, who sent Peter to teach him about Jesus, so that his whole family might be COMFORTED by the Holy Spirit. (Acts 10)

D- Daniel obeyed our DIVINE father, and was DELIVERED from the mouths of lions. God opened DOORS of opportunity for him to serve in captivity. (Dan. 1, 2, 6)

E- Elijah, the prophet who learned about God's love, ENDURED when he fled from King Ahab, and was taken up to heaven by the ETERNAL power of God to be with Him in EVERLASTING life! (I K 18:16-19; II K 2:1-14)

F- The Fisherman, John, the apostle, wrote about FORGIVENESS of sins, and found a FRIEND in Jesus, and a FATHER in God! (John 3:16-21; 20)

G- Gideon was chosen by a GRACIOUS God, who dealt with him GENTLY when he asked for a sign, then helped him lead a handful of men to defeat an army for the GOOD of God's people! (Judges 6-7)

H- Hannah, went to God in prayer for HELP, and our HOLY Father HEALED her barrenness. (I Sam. 1:1- 2:11)

I- Isaiah, the prophet, wrote about the INDESCRIBABLE and INCOMPARABLE plans of our IMMORTAL God. (Isaiah 6; 9:1-7)

J- Joseph, the son of Jacob, found JOY in obeying God, and he learned that the JUDGMENT of God is JUST in all things. (Gen. 45)

K- King David praised his real KING, the Creator, who was KIND to David when he was in hiding and KEPT His promises to David when he ruled Israel. (Psalm 57; Psalm 51)

L- Luke, the physician who accompanied Paul on the missionary journeys, wrote of the LIFE of Jesus and the LIGHT he brought to the world because of God's LOVE for mankind. (Luke 1:1-4; 24)

M- Moses was allowed to come face to face with the MAJESTY of God and to experience the MERCY of our wonderful MASTER! (Ex. 33:12-23; 34:1-35)

N- Noah, a man found worthy in our NOBLE God's sight, was sent to preach NEWS of impending destruction to sinners. But when they still rejected God, God NAVIGATED the ark to save Noah and his family. (Gen. 6- 9:17)

O- Onesimus, Philemon's slave, found comfort in our OMNIPOTENT God, who OPENED His arms and OFFERED His love through Paul, the apostle. (Philemon)

P- Peter, the apostle, was shown the PATIENT love of God when he was allowed to preach the POWERFUL word of God and show the PERFECT way to the first Christians. (Matt. 26:31-35; 69-75; Acts 2:14-41)

Q- Queen Esther was placed in a position to save God's people. God used a QUOTE by Mordecai to encourage her in her fear. He lead her in the QUIET moments and QUICKLY comforted her on her mission. (Esther 4)

R- Ruth followed the RIGHTEOUS God of Abraham and found REFUGE during her struggles and a ROCK to cling to in her future. (Ruth)

S- Samuel, who judged Israel like a SHEPHERD, saw God's SPLENDOR in His choice of David as King and watched as God SAVED Israel from their enemies. (Sam. 16)

T- Timothy, the young evangelist, who allowed God to TENDERLY TEACH him the truth of the gospel through Paul, found that God was TRUSTWORTHY in all situations. (II Tim. 1)

U- The Upright Job, who trusted the one true and UNIQUE God through all of his misery, learned that God's UNDERSTANDING is beyond human understanding and He is UNSURPASSED in His wisdom! (Job 1-2; 42)

V- The Virgin Mary, who found God's will VIRTUOUS, sang a song about His VICTORIOUS deeds, and watched as God was VIGILANT over her son! (Luke1-2)

W- Jesus praised a poor Widow, who gave all she had to God, who is WONDERFUL and WORTHY of praise! In His WISDOM, He knows everything. (Mark 12:41-44)

X- The EXile Ezekiel, who prophesied to the other exiles in Babylon, EXHALTED God and followed His EXTRAORDINARY living examples to tell the people of God's EXCELLENT plans for them! (Ezekiel 4, 37)

Y- The Young men, Shadrach, Meshach, and Abednego, worshipped YAHWEH with all of their hearts, faced a fiery furnace with faith because they understood that YAHWEH YEARNS to save them and YIELDS to no king on earth! (Daniel 3)

Z- Zaccheus, the tax collector, found Jesus as gentle as a ZEPHYR and ZEALOUS to save him. God is the ZENITH, the highest of the high in all things! (Luke 19:2-10)

Printed in the United States
By Bookmasters